Tiny House

15 Great Storing Ideas Expressed in Compact Design + 2 Detailed Plans to Make Them Your Own

Table of Contents

Introduction

You take a look in your garage, and you see tools, a tool chest, camp gear, outdoor items, and the gardening things. Of course there are the random things that you have, too, but where are you supposed to keep those? Then you realize that you have to fit both of your vehicles in there along with any bicycles that you have.

Or perhaps you live in a flat above a downtown street. You don't own a car because everything is right there where you need it, but you do have your bike, and you don't want to leave it outside when the people are all over the place. It is your only form of transportation, and you don't want to risk it getting stolen.

Or perhaps you share your apartment with a roommate. Or two, or three. You have all of your things, and so do they, and there just never seems to be enough storage areas for you to keep everything that you want to keep. You know that you can't rent more storage space, but what are you going to do with it?

You need to have your things, but you also want to enjoy the things that you have indoors. You like to have your space, and it isn't much of a space if it is cluttered beyond function with all of the other things that you have in place. I know that this can be frustrating, but I am here to help you.

It is my goal to see you succeed in this, and to enjoy all of the things that you have, and not have to worry about where you are going to put it. I know that you want to rest easy with it all safe and sound where it should be, but that can be hard when you don't have a lot of space to put it in.

That is why I have put together this book, where you are going to find all of the tips and tricks that you need to effectively store everything that you have. You aren't going to have to worry about a garage sale anymore, or that anyone is going to come up and take what you have when you are asleep.

With these ideas, you are going to have the room to live in your house like you want to, and you can keep all of your things in there, too. Get ready to learn how to decorate in a whole new way, and see the space that you have as potential for even greater things.

It's your space, so make the most of it.

Chapter 1 – Studio Living

If you are in college, a big city, or just like the feel of compact space, it is likely that you are living in a studio. These are some of the best and most economical ways to live, as all of your things are right there in front of you.

The drawback to a studio is the storage, or lack thereof. I am now going to show you the three biggest things that you can do that is going to reinvent the way you think about your studio apartment. All of a sudden, it is going to feel like you have so much more room than you thought you did, and you are going to be able to fit even more things in there.

You can once again think about keeping your things, and hosting that party. It is the best of both worlds.

Use the ceiling

The ceiling is the size of your apartment, it is just above you. There is so much potential space up there that is just waiting to be used, and you are free to use it. Get yourself a stud finder, and you can hang anything you want up there.

Try your bike, your kayak, your hammock, anything that you want you can put up there and secure it in place with hooks and screws. This is going to open up all that room down below, and it is going to look stylish, too.

A complete win all-around for anyone with a lot of large items and not a lot of room. When in doubt, head up the walls, and you are going to be safe.

Closets are for storage first, clothes second

We all have the tendency to put our clothes in the closet, but then we don't know what we are going to do with all of the boxes that are in the living room. I am going to tell you something right now that is going to blow your mind.

No one minds looking at your laundry. If you put your hamper at the foot of your bed, you are going to be just as sexy to that girl you brought home as you would be if you left it in the closet. What you need to do is put away the things that people don't like to look at, and keep out the things that they don't care about.

If you were to walk into a room and it was filled with boxes, you would have a hard time relaxing because you would feel like you were on the move. It would be hard to sit down and forget about things, but if you were to walk into the same room and there was clothing neatly folded off to the side, you wouldn't think anything of it.

Pick and choose the things you are leaving on display, and make the most of a closed door.

Use every bit of space that you can think of

When you are living in a studio, space is precious, this means that you need to use the space that you have. All of it. This includes the cupboards, the space under the couch, under your bed, under the nightstand.

All of it. If you see open space, you can use it. It doesn't matter if it is up, down, beside, or whatever. You are going to become a master at making it fit, and that is a skill that is going to come in handy when you see all of the things that you need to make fit.

Have fun with it and see how creative you can be. There is a lot of different ways you can do it, you just need to use your imagination. Sort of like putting together a puzzle.

Chapter 2 – Shared Space Accommodations

While many of us would rather live alone, it isn't at all unusual to share your space with someone. That could be your sibling, your spouse, or your roommate. This means that you have the same amount of space, but you have to get that much more into it.

Don't worry, there is a lot that you can do when it comes to fitting everyone in nice and neat. You simply need to follow the same rule that you did if you were to live in a studio, but you have to be a little bit more creative.

Make rooms with room dividers

It is true that the size of the room doesn't matter so much as how it looks, and for many, simply putting up a room divider does a lot when it comes to the storage side of things. You can stack up all kinds of boxes, then put a room divider in front of them, and you have instant storage.

What makes this even better is that you can move it around, and mix it up as needed. You might be a person of change, or you might just like to see how it looks differently every now and then.

When you are using room dividers with your boxes, you have all kinds of new potential open up to you, and all you have to do is set it up in front of the boxes that you don't want to see.

Set boundaries and keep your space

With shared space, no matter what the situation is, you need to have your own. This is the best way to keep the peace, and the best way to make it bearable for everyone. To do this, you need to discuss up front what space is yours, then you need to make the most of it.

If you were given a closet, use that for storage, it is your space, so it doesn't matter what you do with it. Again, choose what you would rather look at, and roll with that. If you were given the ceiling, hang stuff like your life depends on it. You might have been given a room or a portion of a room. Make the most of it.

What I am trying to convey here is that you can use the space that you have, and not worry about what that space is. If you can see it, you can use it. Go up, over, under, beside. That is your goal, and that is what is going to save you.

Consolidate whenever possible

Whether it is your stuff, or your roommate's you need to consolidate if you want to keep things as compact as possible. Put all of the things that you can into a single box, and go from there.

You can stack box after box in a closet, but it is going to be a lot easier to get a few heavy boxes into a closet than it would be to get a lot of lighter boxes into a closet. The more that you can get into a single space, the better.

Use markers to label and keep things separate in the closet if you need to, but if there is any way that you can put it all in one, then go with that. You are going to save so much space that you will likely forget that it was even an issue in the first place.

Chapter 3 – Gleaning the Garage

The garage is one of the worst places that we have when it comes to saving space and organizing. Nobody wants to deal with the garage, and when it comes to all of the things that you have out there, who wants to deal with that?

Follow these tips to make the most of your garage, and the things that you have out there. You are going to be so glad that you organized when summer gets here and all you have to do is open a drawer to get out your gardening things.

The little bit of extra work that you put into it right now is going to save you all kinds of work later on down the road.

Set up shelves like it is the last thing you will ever do

When you are saving space in the garage, there is no such thing as too many shelves. Shelves are the savior of the storage world, you can put so many things on them, you can put them close together, and you have countless places that you can keep it.

Hang shelves like you are going to put everything you have in the garage on a shelf, and use every part of the garage that you can. Even the corners are a good place to put things, it frees up a lot of space, and you can stack them close together if you don't have tall things to put on them.

No matter what you have in your garage, you better have at least two of the walls dedicated to shelving.

Organize and use the walls

Staying with the wall trend, you need to put things on the walls as much as possible. Remember that this is your garage and as such you don't need to worry so much about the looks.

Organization and the access are the two most important things that you need to worry about, so put things in categories, and hang them up accordingly. If you can get it up, then do it. Don't worry about how it looks so much as how little space you can get it to use, and you are going to be golden.

You can also use the ceiling of your garage by way of rafters and other shelving up there. I thought that you could infer that from what I was saying, but it seemed like it was a good point to bring up.

Recycle furniture to save space

Don't toss out the old dresser, use it to keep tools and other items in. You can keep all of your garden seeds in a night stand, and a book shelf is the perfect place to keep all of the little things that you don't want to lose when you are out there working.

Be creative and recycle the furniture in your home before you throw it away, this is going to save you a lot of space later on, and it is going to save you a lot of trouble in organization.

Chapter 4 – The Kid's Things

You may have heard that as soon as you have kids, your house is no longer your own, but that is not true, you can get the kids in on the fun, and you can get them to join in with all of the decorating with purpose.

Use your skills when it comes to the children's things as well, and you are going to see that your house doesn't need to be taken over with the kid's things. Here are a few ways you can bring the organization to them, and watch how they join in on the fun.

Corners are all kinds of open space

Hang shelves and nets in corners, and you have the perfect place to keep all of the little stuffed things that your children love. You can toss all of the stuffed animals in their corner net, and you child is going to have a fun way to keep the floor cleaned up.

You can do the same thing when it comes to the special things that they got when they were little that you want to hang onto for a while. Simply put it up in the shelf, and you have an instant way to keep it safe, keep it clean, and keep it out of the way while you go through the stage of life you are in right now.

This is the easiest way to get your kids to actually want to clean their room, no hassle, and no bickering.

Multi-purpose toy boxes are in

You don't have to have a toy box for each thing, you can make a single toy box that does it all. Try adding in little panels into the lid so they can slide their books in and out of it, try adding in a little slide out drawer on the bottom for those Legos and hot wheels.

There are all kinds of ways you can customize a toy chest to accommodate anything that your little one likes, and you are going to fall in love with how easy it is to keep it all straight. Imagine having a single spot for all of the toys and playthings to go.

When you get the whole family in on the organization, you aren't going to have a problem sticking with it yourself. So don't hesitate to make it work for everyone. They are going to love always knowing where everything is, too.

Give everyone a spot, and assign them that spot

Put name tags on hooks on the coat rack, or slots on the shoe rack. If you do this, you are going to have the perfect place to keep everyone's things. If you make them in charge of their spot, you don't have to worry about it getting destroyed, either.

Tell everyone that they have their own special place, and from now on, they are in charge of keeping their things in their space, and keeping them looking nice. This is going to prevent you from ever having to chase down missing shoes, or having a coat rack that is a disaster ever again.

Kids love to help out, and they really like to have responsibility. Your whole family is going to benefit from your kids having their own place to take care of, and you are going to enjoy not having all of the burden fall to you.

Chapter 5 – All Over Tips and Tricks

I thought that now would be a good time to include the tips and tricks that you can use in any room, or for anything. I know that you will always have that last little thing that you aren't sure what to do with, but now you will.

Here are a few tips and tricks that you can use in the garage, in your home, or in your apartment. You are going to find that there is space just waiting to be used everywhere, you just have to know where to look for it, and how to use it.

Stairs are little shelves just waiting to be used

That little space that is under each step is completely empty. You can remove the panel that is covering it, and you have an instant row of shelves that is just waiting to be used.

If you want to get really fancy with it, you can make little drawers that slide in and out of there, and you have the perfect place to keep all of the little hats and mittens that your kids have. You won't ever have to go hunting for those tricky little things again.

And, if you like the look of the knick knacks, you can put them on these shelves. No one plays on the stairs, so you don't have to worry that they are going to get knocked into or broken.

Instant storage, right at your fingertips.

The bathroom can store things, too, you know

Many bathrooms come with a closet or two that is built right in, but these are not really there for any purpose. Sure, you can keep your towels in there, but don't you have enough room under the sink, or don't you have a towel rack?

So many people have what they need right in front of them, but they get trapped with the conventional use of the item and they forget that they can use it for other things that it wasn't supposed to be used for.

Sure, a closet in the bathroom is meant for bathroom things, but who's to say that you can't use it for things like the vacuum? Or how about those boxes you have left over from the move?

There are all kinds of storage opportunities that are just lying about your home, you just have to take the time to look for them. Think outside the box, and you are going to have more room than you ever thought that you had.

Decorate with a purpose

So many times we think that we have to decorate with decorations, and hide the things that aren't, but I want to challenge you to decorate with the things that you use. Hang your dishes on the wall. You can use them for dinner, then hang them up again.

It is multi-purpose decorating, and it is going to save you a lot of space. Who says that you have to store your shoes in your closet? There is all kinds of room right beneath your couch that is just waiting for you to use it. You can just slide a thin piece of plywood beneath there, and you have an instant shoe storage spot.

And the list goes on. I want to challenge you to think outside the box from now on. You can do it, and it is going to give you so many more spots to store that you didn't realize was just sitting around in your home.

So have fun with it and see what else you have waiting for you. When you look at your space with an open mind, and when you are willing to break out of the box that society has you in, you are going to see that there is so much more you can do with your space and your things, and that the space is going to serve you well when it comes to your storage.

Chapter 6 – Making it Your Own

You have probably gotten so many ideas from the above listings that you are ready to try it out and make them your own, but I want to show you a couple of things before I send you out into the lion's den.

If you are going to use any of these projects for your own home, there are some definite things that you want to keep in mind. These are things that beginners often overlook, and pay the consequences for later on. If you do these right now, you are going to save yourself a lot of headache later on down the road.

Details for your own home, plan 1.

First things first, there are a list of rules that you need to follow when you are doing your own project, and they are slightly varied based on the project that you are doing.

There are, however, some rules that are universal. These are things that you ought to do no matter what your project is or how you are going about doing it. These are:

1. Clear your work space – you can't work where there is clutter, debris, toys, other people, pets, or anything that is going to get in your way. Clean it up and start from there.

2. Gather all of the tools you need in advance – there are few things that are more frustrating than when you are halfway through a project and you run into issues. Either you don't have what you need, or you run into things that you weren't expecting, and can't go on until they are resolved. If you make a list of the things that you need in advance, you are going to bypass this unfortunate delay and things are going to go a lot smoother.

3. Have an end goal in mind – in other words, you want to know what you are shooting for. If you want to get your kayak off of the floor, then work with that end goal in mind. If you just want to get things cleaned up, then you are going to need to make a list of the end goals that you want in the beginning, then base your work off of that.

4. Get rid of the extra clutter – this book is designed to help you use the space you have to store the things that you care about. With that being said, we can infer that there are things that you don't care about, and these are things that are using up space that you need for other items. Get rid of them and use the space that they open up.

5. Be bold – this is another thing that a lot of people hesitate to do. If you want to do something big, go for it. It is your house and your space, so don't worry about what the neighbors think, you can do what you want, and if it is safe and saving you money, then what is holding you back?

Before you begin any do-it-yourself projects, make sure that you go through the details of this plan and prepare. A little bit of work in advance is going to save you a whole bunch of work later on down the road.

You are setting up your life to be efficient and smooth, so start now with the small things, you can worry about the finer details later on.

Details for your own home, plan 2.

Now that you have gone through the first plan, you have all of the prep work done. This means that you have reached the exciting part, which is the 'doing' of your project.

You can plan and plan all you want, but until you are in the part where you are actually doing what you planned, you aren't really getting anywhere. Get all of the pre-stuff done, and you are going to be ready for this second plan.

1. Gather the tools that you need and keep them organized and within reach

2. Make sure you have someone who knows what you are doing if you are working with heavy or dangerous items. Safety first.

3. Draw up your project management plan- if you don't know what this is, the name says it all. You plan out the work as you are going to do it, then

you follow that. If you are in a time limit, you can decide how long each part of the project should take you, and aim for those goals.

Doing this keeps you on track and makes sure everything is going along as it should.

4. Innovate and improvise – don't be afraid to pull out the power tools and get down and dirty with it. You know how you want this to look when it is done, and there are only so many boxes that you can stack on top of each other before you really need to pull in the big guns.

5. If you don't like it, move it around more – you aren't trapped with anything that you decide to do. If you do something and you don't like how it turns out, simply change it around and do it another way. Again, this is your home, so do what you want. If you like it, then you succeeded.

I hope that these plans were able to help you prepare for your project and execute what you wanted easily. This whole thing shouldn't be that hard for you to do, you just have to do it. I know that in the excitement it can be difficult to actually sit down and do the work, but if you stick with it, you are going to be amazed at what you are able to come up with.

I know that you have the room for all of the things that you want to store, so just get up and do it. You don't have to choose this or that, you can have both.

If you work hard and do your best to make it work, odds are it is going to work.

Good luck and happy renovating!

Conclusion

There you have it, everything that you need to know to decorate your space and make the most out of what you have available to you. I hope that with this book you are able to see how you can use space that you never thought of using before, and that you can choose how to store things wisely rather than having to get rid of the things that you have.

The next thing that you need to do is practice what you have learned. It is unlikely that you now own everything that you ever will own, and I don't want you to find yourself in this situation again later on down the road, so make sure you apply what you have learned, and that you use it when you get more things.

Show your friends how to do it, and you are going to be amazed at how much room you can utilize for your storage and not have to worry about it not looking good. I hope you are able to get all of your things into your space with ease, and I assure you that with a little practice, you are going to get what you want out of the space that you have.

Learn how to appreciate the space that you have, and you are going to see so much more potential with all of the space that is around you. There is a new way to decorating, and you have discovered what you need to make it all work out the best way possible.

Happy storing!

FREE Bonus Reminder

If you have not grabbed it yet, please go ahead and download your special bonus report *"DIY Projects. 13 Useful & Easy To Make DIY Projects To Save Money & Improve Your Home!"*

Simply Click the Button Below

OR **Go to This Page**

http://diyhomecraft.com/free

BONUS #2: More Free Books

Do you want to receive more Free Books?

We have a mailing list where we send out our new Books when they go free on Kindle. Click on the link below to sign up for Free Book Promotions.

=> Sign Up for Free Book Promotions <=

OR Go to this URL

http://zbit.ly/1WBb1Ek